HAL•LEONARD

BASS PLAY-ALONG

AUDIO ACCESS INCLUDED

SONGS FOR BEGINNERS

Play 8 Songs with Tab and Sound-alike Audio

PLAYBACK+
Speed • Pitch • Balance • Loop

To access audio visit:
www.halleonard.com/mylibrary

Enter Code
3988-0863-8040-1648

ISBN 978-1-5400-9408-7

Visit Hal Leonard Online at
www.halleonard.com

Contact us:
Hal Leonard
7777 West Bluemound Road
Milwaukee, WI 53213
Email: info@halleonard.com

In Europe, contact:
Hal Leonard Europe Limited
42 Wigmore Street
Marylebone, London, W1U 2RN
Email: info@halleonardeurope.com

In Australia, contact:
Hal Leonard Australia Pty. Ltd.
4 Lentara Court
Cheltenham, Victoria, 3192 Australia
Email: info@halleonard.com.au

BASS NOTATION LEGEND

Bass music can be notated two different ways: on a *musical staff*, and in *tablature*

THE MUSICAL STAFF shows pitches and rhythms and is divided by bar lines into measures. Pitches are named after the first seven letters of the alphabet.

TABLATURE graphically represents the bass fingerboard. Each horizontal line represents a string, and each number represents a fret.

Notes:

Strings:

3rd string, open   2nd string, 2nd fret   1st & 2nd strings open, played together

HAMMER-ON: Strike the first (lower) note with one finger, then sound the higher note (on the same string) with another finger by fretting it without picking.

PULL-OFF: Place both fingers on the notes to be sounded. Strike the first note and without picking, pull the finger off to sound the second (lower) note.

LEGATO SLIDE: Strike the first note and then slide the same fret-hand finger up or down to the second note. The second note is not struck.

SHIFT SLIDE: Same as legato slide, except the second note is struck.

TRILL: Very rapidly alternate between the notes indicated by continuously hammering on and pulling off.

TREMOLO PICKING: The note is picked as rapidly and continuously as possible.

VIBRATO: The string is vibrated by rapidly bending and releasing the note with the fretting hand.

SHAKE: Using one finger, rapidly alternate between two notes on one string by sliding either a half-step above or below.

NATURAL HARMONIC: Strike the note while the fret hand lightly touches the string directly over the fret indicated.

MUFFLED STRINGS: A percussive sound is produced by laying the fret hand across the string(s) without depressing them and striking them with the pick hand.

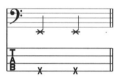

BEND: Strike the note and bend up the interval shown.

BEND AND RELEASE: Strike the note and bend up as indicated, then release back to the original note. Only the first note is struck.

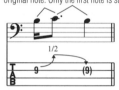

RIGHT-HAND TAP: Hammer ("tap") the fret indicated with the "pick-hand" index or middle finger and pull off to the note fretted by the fret hand.

LEFT-HAND TAP: Hammer ("tap") the fret indicated with the "fret-hand" index or middle finger.

SLAP: Strike ("slap") string with right-hand thumb.

POP: Snap ("pop") string with right-hand index or middle finger.

Additional Musical Definitions

 (accent)   • Accentuate note (play it louder)

 (accent)   • Accentuate note with great intensity

 (staccato)   • Play the note short

D.S. al Coda   • Go back to the sign (𝄋), then play until the measure marked ***"To Coda"***, then skip to the section labelled ***"Coda."***

Fill   • Label used to identify a brief pattern which is to be inserted into the arrangement.

    • Repeat measures between signs.

   • When a repeated section has different endings, play the first ending only the first time and the second ending only the second time.

All Star

from the DreamWorks Motion Picture SHREK

Words and Music by Greg Camp

Tune down 1/2 step:
(low to high) E♭-A♭-D♭-G♭

Verse
Moderately ♩ = 104

1. Some - bod - y once told me the world __ is gon - na roll me; I ain't the sharp - est tool in the shed. __

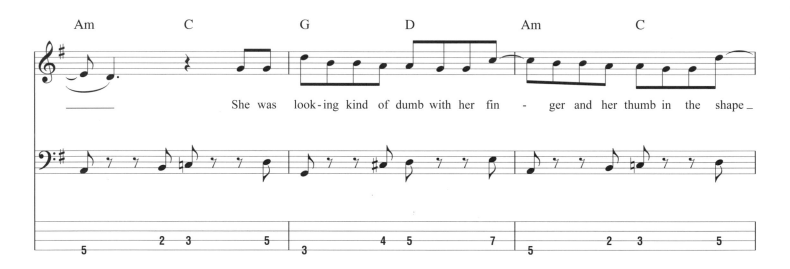

__ She was look - ing kind of dumb with her fin - ger and her thumb in the shape __

__ of an "L" __ on her fore - head. 2. Well, the

Verse

years start com-ing and they don't stop com-ing.   Fed   to   the   rules,   and   I   hit   the   ground   run-ning.
3. *See additional lyrics*

Did-n't make sense   not to live   for fun.   Your brain gets smart, but your head gets   dumb. __

So much   to do,   so   much __ to see.   So what's wrong __ with tak - ing   the back streets?   You'll

nev - er know   if you don't   go.   You'll   nev - er shine   if   you don't   glow.

Additional Lyrics

3. It's a cool place, and they say it gets colder.
   You're bundled up now; wait till you get older.
   But the meteor men beg to differ,
   Judging by the hole in the satellite picture.
   The ice we skate is getting pretty thin.
   The water's getting warm so you might as well swim.
   My world's on fire. How 'bout yours?
   That's the way I like it and I'll never get bored.

Boulevard of Broken Dreams

Words by Billie Joe
Music by Green Day

Intro
Moderately slow ♩ = 84

Bass tacet

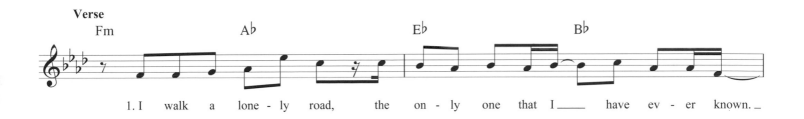

Verse

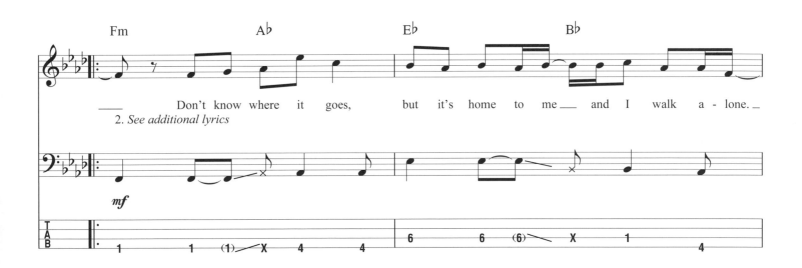

1. I walk a lone-ly road, the on-ly one that I ___ have ev - er known. ___

Don't know where it goes, but it's home to me ___ and I walk a - lone. ___
2. *See additional lyrics*

mf

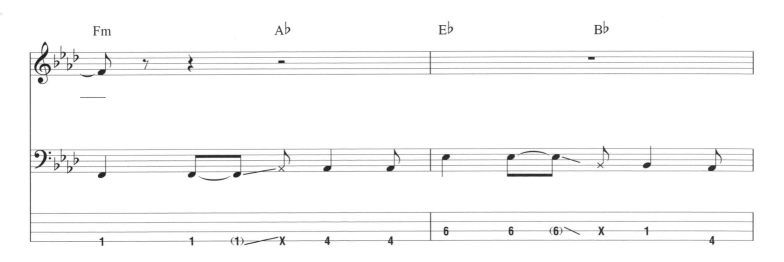

Additional Lyrics

2. I'm walkin' down the line that divides me somewhere in my mind.
On the borderline of the edge and where I walk alone.
Read between the lines, what's fucked up and ev'rything's alright.
Check my vital signs to know I'm still alive and I walk alone.
I walk alone, I walk alone.
I walk alone, I walk a...

Cake by the Ocean

Words and Music by Joseph Jonas, Justin Tranter, Robin Fredriksson and Mattias Larsson

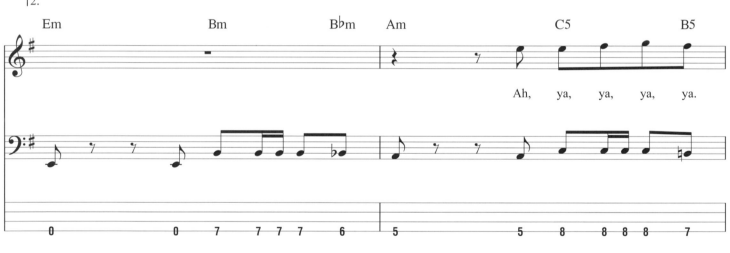

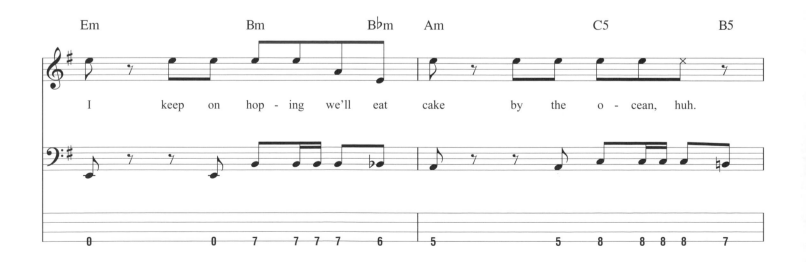

Ah, ya, ya, ya, ya.

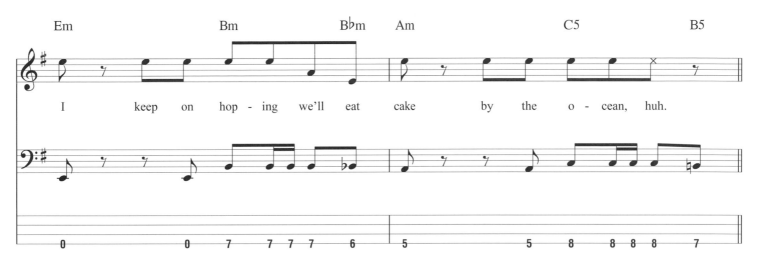

I keep on hop - ing we'll eat cake by the o - cean, huh.

Interlude

D.S. al Coda

Bass tacet

Hey. You're fuck-in' de - li - cious. Ha, ha, ha. Talk to me, girl. __

Coda

Outro

Red vel - vet, va - nil - la, choc - 'late in my life. __

Additional Lyrics

2. God damn! See you lickin' frosting from your own hands.
Want another taste? I'm beggin', "Yes, ma'am."
I'm tired of all this candy on the dry land, dry land, oh.

My Own Worst Enemy

Words and Music by Jeremy Popoff, Jay Popoff, Kevin Baldes and Allen Shellenberger

Tune down 1/2 step:
(low to high) Eb-Ab-Db-Gb

Intro
Moderately ♩ = 104

(Guitar)

1. Can we for-get __ a - bout __ the things __ I said __ when I __ was drunk? __
2. *See additional lyrics*

I did - n't mean __ to call __ you that. __

Additional Lyrics

2. It's no surprise to me, I am my own worst enemy.
   'Cause ev'ry now and then I kick the living shit outta me.
   The smoke alarm is goin' off and there's a cigarette
   Still burnin'. Please tell me why...

Can't Stop the Feeling!

from TROLLS

Words and Music by Justin Timberlake, Max Martin and Shellback

Intro
Moderately ♩ = 112

Bass tacet

1. I've got this feel-ing inside my bones. It goes e-
2. *See additional lyrics*

lec-tric, wav-y when I turn it on. All through my cit-y, all through my

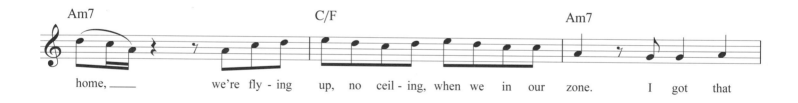

home, _____ we're fly-ing up, no ceil-ing, when we in our zone. I got that

sun-shine in my pock-et, got that good soul in my feet. I feel that

Additional Lyrics

2. Ooh, it's something magical.
It's in the air, it's in my blood, it's rushing on.
I don't need no reason, don't need control.
I fly so high, no ceiling, when I'm in my zone.
'Cause I got that...

Castle on the Hill

Words and Music by Ed Sheeran and Benjamin Levin

*Guitar arr. for bass, next 8 meas.

Interlude

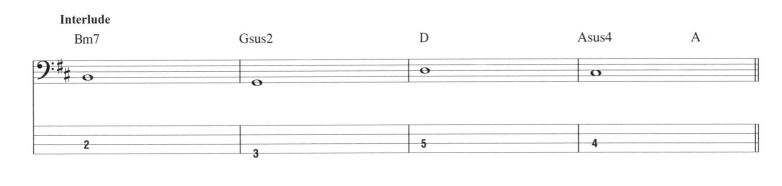

Bridge

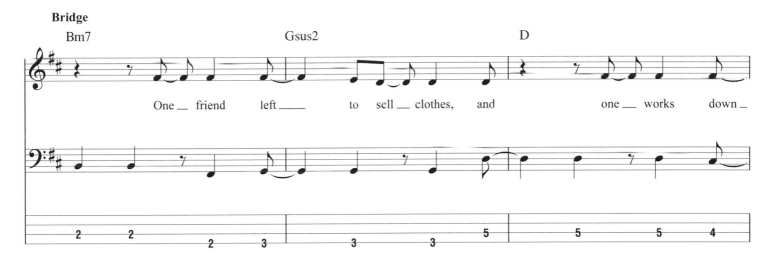

One — friend left —— to sell — clothes, and one — works down —

—— by — the coast. One had — two kids —— but lives a - lone.

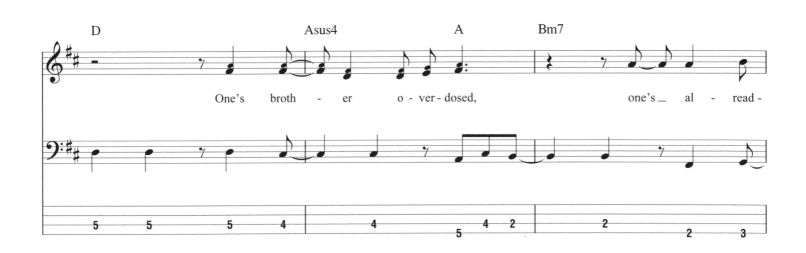

One's broth - er o - ver - dosed, one's — al - read -

Creep

Words and Music by Albert Hammond, Mike Hazlewood, Thomas Yorke,
Jonathan Greenwood, Colin Greenwood, Edward O'Brien and Philip Selway

2nd time, substitute Fill 2

2nd time, substitute Fill 3

-cial.   You're so fuck-ing spe - cial, _____

Chorus

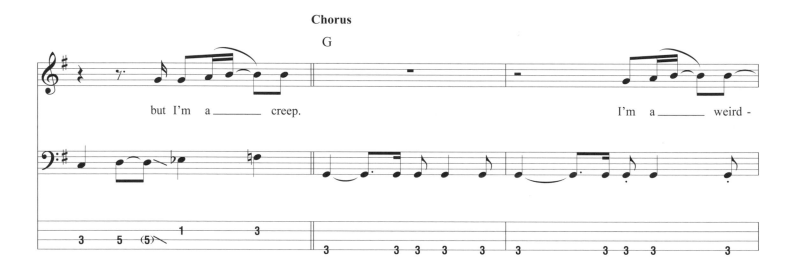

but I'm a _____ creep.   I'm a _____ weird-

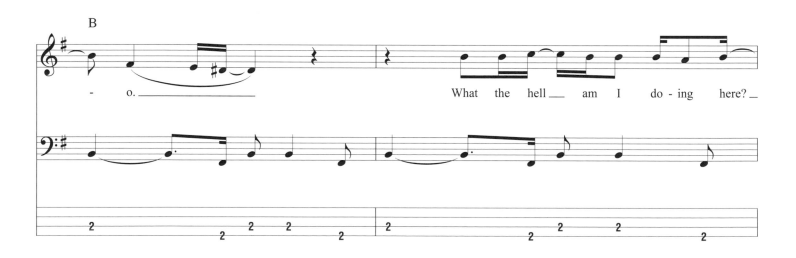

-o. _____   What the hell __ am I do-ing here? __

Fill 3

run,   run,   run,   run. _____

Run. _____

Verse

3. What-ev-er makes you hap - py.   What-ev-er you want. __

Additional Lyrics

2. I don't care if it hurts, I wanna have control.
   I want a perfect body. I want a perfect soul.
   I want you to notice when I'm not around.
   You're so fucking special. I wish I was special,
   But I'm a creep.

Seven Nation Army

Words and Music by Jack White

To Coda 1 ⊕

Interlude

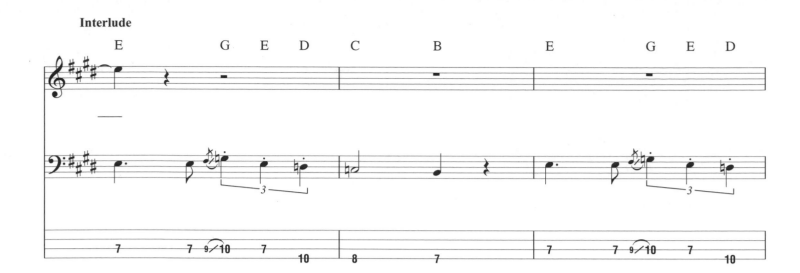

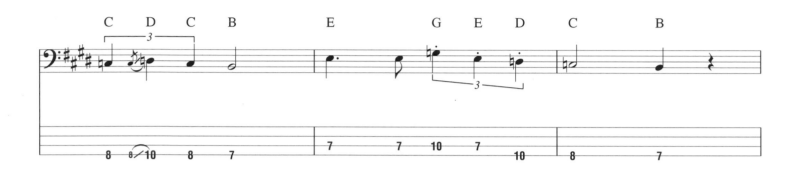

To Coda 2 ⊕

D.C. al Coda 1
(take repeats)

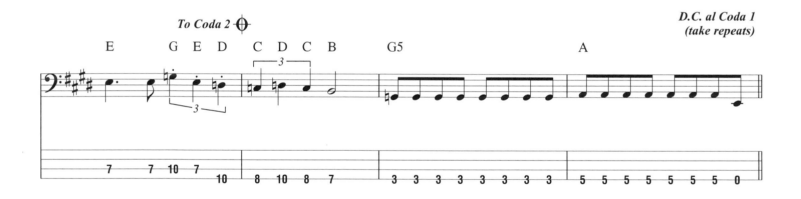

 Coda 1

Guitar Solo

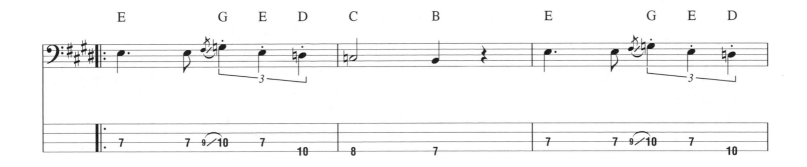

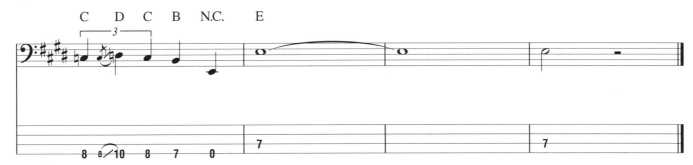

D.C. al Coda 2
(take repeats)

Additional Lyrics

2. Don't wanna hear about it, ev'ry single one's got a story to tell.
Ev'ryone knows about it, from the Queen of England to the hounds of hell.
And if I catch it coming back my way, I'm gonna serve it to you.
And that ain't what you want to hear, but that's what I'll do.
And the feeling coming from my bones says find a home.

3. I'm goin' to Wichita, far from this opera forevermore.
I'm gonna work the straw, make the sweat drip out of every pore.
And I'm bleeding, and I'm bleeding, and I'm bleeding right before the Lord.
All the words are gonna bleed from me and I will think no more.
And the stains coming from my blood tell me go back home.

HAL•LEONARD® BASS PLAY-ALONG

The Bass Play-Along™ Series will help you play your favorite songs quickly and easily! Just follow the tab, listen to the audio to hear how the bass should sound, and then play-along using the separate backing tracks. The melody and lyrics are also included in the book in case you want to sing, or to simply help you follow along. The audio files are enhanced so you can adjust the recording to any tempo without changing pitch!

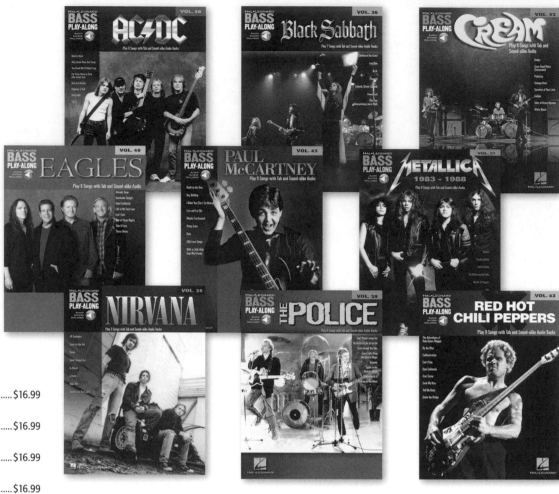

1. Rock
00699674 Book/Online Audio $16.99

2. R&B
00699675 Book/Online Audio $16.99

3. Songs for Beginners
00346426 Book/Online Audio $16.99

4. '90s Rock
00294992 Book/Online Audio $16.99

5. Funk
00699680 Book/Online Audio $16.99

6. Classic Rock
00699678 Book/Online Audio $17.99

8. Punk Rock
00699813 Book/CD Pack $12.95

9. Blues
00699817 Book/Online Audio $16.99

10. Jimi Hendrix – Smash Hits
00699815 Book/Online Audio $17.99

11. Country
00699818 Book/CD Pack $12.95

12. Punk Classics
00699814 Book/CD Pack $12.99

13. The Beatles
00275504 Book/Online Audio $16.99

14. Modern Rock
00699821 Book/CD Pack $14.99

15. Mainstream Rock
00699822 Book/CD Pack $14.99

16. '80s Metal
00699825 Book/CD Pack $16.99

17. Pop Metal
00699826 Book/CD Pack $14.99

18. Blues Rock
00699828 Book/CD Pack $19.99

19. Steely Dan
00700203 Book/Online Audio $17.99

20. The Police
00700270 Book/Online Audio $19.99

21. Metallica: 1983-1988
00234338 Book/Online Audio $19.99

22. Metallica: 1991-2016
00234339 Book/Online Audio $19.99

23. Pink Floyd – Dark Side of The Moon
00700847 Book/Online Audio $16.99

24. Weezer
00700960 Book/CD Pack $17.99

25. Nirvana
00701047 Book/Online Audio $17.99

26. Black Sabbath
00701180 Book/Online Audio $17.99

27. Kiss
00701181 Book/Online Audio $17.99

28. The Who
00701182 Book/Online Audio $19.99

29. Eric Clapton
00701183 Book/Online Audio $15.99

30. Early Rock
00701184 Book/CD Pack $15.99

31. The 1970s
00701185 Book/CD Pack $14.99

32. Cover Band Hits
00211598 Book/Online Audio $16.99

33. Christmas Hits
00701197 Book/CD Pack $12.99

34. Easy Songs
00701480 Book/Online Audio $17.99

35. Bob Marley
00701702 Book/Online Audio $17.99

36. Aerosmith
00701886 Book/CD Pack $14.99

37. Modern Worship
00701920 Book/Online Audio $19.99

38. Avenged Sevenfold
00702386 Book/CD Pack $16.99

39. Queen
00702387 Book/Online Audio $17.99

40. AC/DC
14041594 Book/Online Audio $17.99

41. U2
00702582 Book/Online Audio $19.99

42. Red Hot Chili Peppers
00702991 Book/Online Audio $19.99

43. Paul McCartney
00703079 Book/Online Audio $17.99

44. Megadeth
00703080 Book/CD Pack $16.99

45. Slipknot
00703201 Book/CD Pack $17.99

46. Best Bass Lines Ever
00103359 Book/Online Audio $19.99

47. Dream Theater
00111940 Book/Online Audio $24.99

48. James Brown
00117421 Book/CD Pack $16.99

49. Eagles
00119936 Book/Online Audio $17.99

50. Jaco Pastorius
00128407 Book/Online Audio $17.99

51. Stevie Ray Vaughan
00146154 Book/CD Pack $16.99

52. Cream
00146159 Book/Online Audio $17.99

56. Bob Seger
00275503 Book/Online Audio $16.99

57. Iron Maiden
00278398 Book/Online Audio $17.99

58. Southern Rock
00278436 Book/Online Audio $17.99

HAL•LEONARD®

Prices, contents, and availability subject to change without notice.

Visit Hal Leonard Online at **www.halleonard.com**